# Charisma:

## 7 Ways to Develop Genuine Charisma, Social Skills & Increase Your Confidence

## Copyright Notice

No part of this book may be reproduced or transmitted in any form whatsoever, electronic, or mechanical, including photocopying, recording, or by any information storage or retrieval system without expressed written, dated and signed permission from the author. All copyrights are reserved.

## Disclaimer

Reasonable care has been taken to ensure that the information presented in this book is accurate. However, the reader should understand that the information provided does not constitute legal, medical or professional advice of any kind.

No Liability: this product is supplied "as is" and without warranties. All warranties, express or implied, are hereby disclaimed. Use of this product constitutes acceptance of the "No Liability" policy. If you do not agree with this policy, you are not permitted to use or distribute this product.

We shall not be liable for any losses or damages whatsoever (including, without limitation, consequential loss or damage) directly or indirectly arising from the use of this product.

# Buyer Bonus:

## Rituals Of The Rich & Famous

Free Access to Success Tips, Strategies and Habits of The Rich & Famous

Join successful subscribers!

Get 4 new strategies every week on how to be more charismatic, confident, and happy.

### Free Sign Up Here

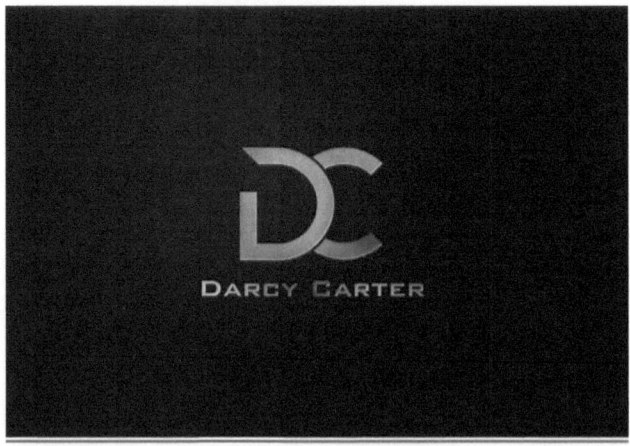

# **Buyer Bonus 2**

## **Attachment Theory, The Science of Successful Relationships, Authentic Love, Romance and Connection**

Discover the secrets to building healthy, happy, and rewarding relationships.

The key ingredient to happy and fulfilled people is the quality of their intimate, social, family, and professional relationships - nothing else in life comes even remotely close.

Go ahead, transform the quality of your relationships and make love work for you.

# ATTACHMENT THEORY

*The Science of Successful Relationships, Authentic, Love, Romance and Connection*

## DARCY CARTER

# Contents

**Introduction**

**Chapter 1 - Be Authentic**

**Chapter 2 - Build Your Self-Image**

**Chapter 3 - Be Energetic**

**Chapter 4 - Cherish Similarities and Honor Differences**

**Chapter 5 - Give Value**

**Chapter 6 - Be Memorable**

**Conclusion**

**Buyer Bonus:**

**Buyer Bonus 2**

# Introduction

Charisma is seen as a key aspect of a great personality.

The ability to delight and charm other people - to be funny, to be interesting, to be disarming - is a valuable trait that you can develop and will help you in your personal and business relationships.

Perhaps you have learned from "personality gurus" that you can fake charisma using certain strategies used by celebrities, leaders, and keynote speakers. But unfortunately, this is far from the truth.

Enhancing your charisma doesn't mean you need to be always happy or making everything bright and perky. In fact, there are situations that you may need to do the opposite.

Improving your likability is about exploring what is genuinely likable in you, in the people around you, and in your relationships. It is via the strength of authenticity that valuable networks can become meaningful relationships.

For you to boost your charisma, you need to understand its nature and dynamics. We have our unique personalities, which makes it really exciting to explore the social sphere. We have our own charisma, but still, the fundamental drivers of likability are the same for everyone.

In this book, we will take a closer look at specific ways that can help you improve your likability in both personal and business settings:

- *Authenticity*
- *Self-Perception*
- *Energy*
- *Curiosity*
- *Similarities and Differences*
- *Value*
- *Mood Memory*

These methods for connecting with people you like will provide you to grab more opportunities and nurture your social life. By studying these methods, you will discover what is naturally likable about yourself, and how you can share these qualities with the people you meet to build relationships that are genuine.

By enhancing your charisma, you can help yourself to be more successful, more comfortable, and be generally happier.

Once again, thanks for downloading this book, I hope you find it to be helpful!

# Chapter 1 - Be Authentic

How exactly can a person be more authentic?

The specifics can be different for each of us because we all have different values, goals, knowledge, skill sets, beliefs, behaviors, and attitudes. But in a general sense, authenticity is the same for all of us. Authenticity invokes being natural that when you are true to yourself, you might not even notice it.

On the other hand, you will easily notice when you are not your natural self. You are not comfortable, you feel awkward, maybe stressed and unconfident, and usually after spending a significant amount of time where you are really just faking it, you feel drained - not just tired.

There's a difference between drained and tired.

Being tired is physically manifested but being drained involves mental exhaustion. This feeling of emptiness comes from the emotional or mental effort of exerting energy so you can act in a manner that is really not natural for you.

You can be drained if you are doing something that doesn't really feel right. What is really happening inside your mind when you are not being your true self?

Perhaps, you really don't like socializing at a party, but you are just trying to be polite. Or maybe you don't like a particular person, but you are trying to act cordial.

Some people feel drained all the time because they are forced to act like a successful communicator. They believe that they are not likable if people cannot respond positively to them. Some are really not comfortable in a particular situation and they just don't know what to do.

Most of these reasons really represent things that you feel you are expected to do, or you feel that you are vulnerable. You may put on a mask when, for any reason, you feel you are not up to something or you just dread a specific situation.

Being authentic is not only a particular method to be charismatic, but it is also the overarching theme of this book.

As you read through this book, you will learn that being genuine is a basic element in other ways to enhance your social skills. It is key to charisma because it captures the essence of being likable. Your authentic self is your best self. You will discover that authenticity is a powerful tool in forging genuine relationships with the people you want to attract.

## When Are You Authentic?

In order to identify the specific situations when you can really say that you are authentic, you should explicitly focus on how you feel at the start of a new connection and how you feel at the end.

If you dread a situation, pause and identify what it triggers that uncomfortable feeling. Is it the environment, the task, or the person? If you really like a situation, pause and try to identify what makes you feel comfortable?

Take note of your responses and try to take a closer look at each one. Your responses must disclose important details about the types of experiences that trigger you to shy away from presenting your authentic self as well as those experiences that you feel find it easier to be authentic.

Leverage these self-images about what you naturally feel and consider them as your home base perception where you can return from time to time to really understand what authenticity means for you.

## How to Be Authentic?

Being authentic means presenting who you are - your natural energy and your genuine responses.

Sharing what is authentic about you is the cornerstone of building real connections with other people. Whenever you present your authenticity, people will also respond naturally. This establishes the bedrock for growth, connections, and mutual understanding.

But how can you become authentic?

The great thing about becoming authentic is that it doesn't require a lot of effort. You don't need to go the extra mile because you just need to be.

Yes, it is easy to be authentic, but embracing this principle can be easier said than done.

With our hectic schedules, many of us tend to just hustle through situations without spending too much thought, and so we may not even be conscious when we are and are not being authentic.

Even if we are aware that we are not authentic (whenever we are putting on a mask or just sleepwalking through a situation) it is often not easy to interfere with the behavior.

However, the key is to just stop trying to be who you think you must be and stop premeditating or monitoring your actions. Just be your true self.

Have you ever wondered why reality shows are now such big hits on television? Popular reality shows such as "America's Next Top Model" or "Big Brother" have garnered millions of eyeballs around the world and continue to rake in millions of dollars in revenue.

One reason is that people are just tired of scripted shows and they want to take a peek into the real living situations of models vying to take the next spot in the limelight or witnessing some crazy scenarios involving strangers who are now spending 24/7 with each other inside a house.

So many of these shows will allow you to see primal struggles between personality types, and it can be fascinating to see the dramas play out.

Have you seen how kids behave without any filter? They naturally shine when they are in their authentic selves. While you don't need to be child like, you can use this home base to reconnect with that uncensored experience of being a kid, before adulthood began changing you based on what it perceived to be the bigger world you wanted.

Just try to think back to the time that preceded adult responsibilities and worries to a time when your behaviors, intentions, and emotions were largely unfettered.

Once you are able to establish this primal connection, you can feel at ease. You will soon realize that even though you might dread being part of a large crowd and you are compelled to be the life of the party; you can be totally comfortable in engaging small groups or one-on-one.

Under these controlled settings, you may easily engage people in more meaningful conversations about the things that really matter to you most.

## The Test for Authenticity

Whenever you are in a situation that makes you feel disconnected or uncomfortable, step back and take a closer look if you are being authentic.

If you can say that you are authentic, then sure, continue doing what you are doing. There are instances that being uncomfortable or disconnected could mean that you have to refocus your attention so you can reconnect with the situation with more authenticity.

The discomfort you feel in a particular situation might be caused by pushing yourself affirmatively. Under such circumstances, the discomfort might be part of being genuine.

However, if you believe that you are not authentic in that situation, then you might need to dig deeper to know the deeper reason behind the discomfort or disconnect.

Probably you might be changing your behavior because of how you think you must act. Moreover, there might be something about the situation, which makes you a bit nervous or lacking.

For such scenarios, try to relax and reconnect with that aspect of you that you feel genuine and honest.

Try visualizing the worst case scenario. You will discover that usually, the outcome is not all that bad. Just anchor on your contribution to the situation. Presenting your authentic self will help you in establishing your connection regardless of the result.

## Activity: Reframing Authenticity

You can present your authentic self whenever you make the choices you want to make and not just the ones that you think you should really make.

It's not only about choosing the situations that you want to be part of but deciding how you want to respond to the events as they happen.

You can bring four basic colors to categorize each behavior that you can any situation. This will help reaffirm what is genuine for yourself or help you readjust your approach so you can reveal your authentic self.

Red

The color red pertains to what the community, your company, or some other external forces think what you should do. While you may agree with some of them, these are the things that you wouldn't want to do, but rather what you feel you are obliged to do.

## Orange

This refers to the things you really dread, although you understand the importance of accomplishing them.

## Green

This refers to the things that you really want to do, although choosing and doing them is often difficult for you.

## Blue

This refers to the things that make you really excited, alert, and genuinely giddy.

As a quick assessment, select anything from your daily tasks or your calendar of activities, and then promptly, without too much thinking, select the right color that is most appropriate for each task.

You might be surprised by how much this basic exercise will reveal. For example, if you have an upcoming presentation with an important client, you could find yourself thinking that you have to persuade the boss of a big corporation, or you have to persuade a client that can save your business.

Notice that even if you need to deal with the same situation, you can change your perception towards it. Same situation, different attitudes. Once you determine what your attitude is, you can consider your options and decide what to do about it.

Your first option is to pursue the activity if you tagged as blue or green because it will become effortless for you. If you tagged the pitch as orange or red then you have to determine how to get over it if the task is crucial even if the authentic desire to do it is not really present. In these scenarios, find a way to complete the task that will allow you to be genuine with yourself.

Chances are, your job entails attending meetings and mingling with clients and coworkers. This might be a key part of your job regardless of how uncomfortable it is for you.

But instead of imposing an inauthentic role on yourself or trying to be the life of the party, you can instead choose to talk with smaller groups, that can make you more effective and comfortable. You can still do things that you dread but are important without compromising your authenticity.

Another option is to reframe your mindset. There are instances that it is powerful and possible to approach a situation from a new perspective, which could literally change the way you perceive it.

For example, if your original attitude towards a client pitch was "I have to attend a pitch and persuade this client," you can reframe it by saying "I want to share our service that can really help this client increase his sales."

By reframing a challenging situation, you can focus on the characteristics of it that can make you feel energized and good. With this, you can recast the activity as green or blue.

There are instances that you don't have any option left but to avoid the situation. But take note that it is not always easy to just let go of an activity. There are certain activities that should be completed, and in these activities, you have to put on your best effort.

Before you let go of activities that you have tagged as red or orange, it pays well if you take a second look at them. Sometimes, people have a tendency to be deeply ingrained in the red or orange mentality that it could dominate our thinking and really cloud our judgement to the point where we might just give up.

However, if you think that a red or orange activity is not really important, and that completing it is just for compliance, then let it go. If you are not capable of working on the task with your full energy and authenticity, then you may not make the best use of your time or yourself.

## Common Bad Habits that Make People Instantly Dislike You

The first impression really lasts, and it may not take more than three minutes to make someone realize that they don't want to spend time with you.

Many of the ways that turn people off are caused by lack of authenticity such as the following:

## Hiding Your Real Emotions

Studies show that showing your genuine emotions is a better way to get people like you than hiding them inside.

For example, in one study, researchers videotaped the reactions of people watching a sad scene in the film "The Champ" and the fake orgasm scene in the film "When Harry Met Sally".

In some scenes, the actors were told to naturally react, and in another, they were told to bottle up their emotions. The researchers then presented the four versions of the videos to some college students and measured how much they are interested in befriending the people in the videos.

Results showed that those who suppressed their emotions were perceived as less charismatic compared to people who have shown their natural emotions.

## Telling Secrets to Strangers

Basically, people become more close to each other if they share secrets. As a matter of fact, self-disclosure is one of the best ways to befriend someone.

However, scientists reveal that disclosing something that is too personal such as your cousin having an affair can significantly decrease your likability because you may be perceived as insecure.

There is no need to share intimate secrets to a person whom you really want to be close with. If you are in the early stages of a relationship, you can just share details about your hobbies or your favorite memories. This will make you more likable.

## Being Overly Nice

You may think that you can win people over by becoming too nice, but research suggests otherwise.

In a study conducted at Washington State University in 2010, researchers provided college students with points that they may keep or exchange for meal vouchers.

The participants were oriented that they were playing in five groups, although the other four groups were accomplices who were ordered by the researchers to be overly nice. The actual participants were told that giving up their points would increase the chances of the group to receive cash rewards.

Other fake participants were instructed to give away lots of points and insisted on taking a few meal vouchers. After the activity, most participants said they were not interested to work with their teammates who were unselfish. They thought that the participants who were overly nice had ulterior motives.

So you may think twice about always volunteering to fix the printer or get the pizza. Sometimes, you have to say no but be sure to explain why you can't extend a hand.

## Humblebragging

Humblebragging is the act of criticizing yourself, but actually you are really complimenting. This can turn-off not only your friends but also potential employers.

In one study, researchers asked college students to write down their biggest weakness in the workplace. Results indicated that around 75% of participants answered: "working too hard" or being "perfectionist".

However, independent research assistants said they like the participants who were honest and would be open to hiring them. The responses of the participants were like "there are times that I find myself overreacting" and "It is not easy for me to be organized at work".

To make sure that you ace that classic job interview question, you can talk about your weakness that is not directly related to the job - for instance, a fear of selling to people if you're applying for a video editor position.

## Introverted Authenticity

Many introverts think that building relationships and forging connections come easily with extroverts. Most extroverts cannot confirm or deny this as they usually don't think too much about it as they are quite busy being genuine that they often ignore the need to pause and assess what they are doing.

But as a matter of fact, extroverts also face their own challenges when it comes to building relationships as you will later learn in this book.

If you are an introvert, you should know that you can still be comfortable in social and business situations. Being introverted doesn't mean you are weak.

More often than not, introverts are naturally capable of initiating connections because they have great listening skills.

If you are introverted, it is important for you to listen to your own rhythms and don't worry about sounding like your extroverted friends. Focus on the things that you are most comfortable doing. For instance, if you're exhausted, you can simply leave a gathering or a party so you can rest. You don't have to "go with what your friends would want you to do".

When you are with a group of people, do you opt to be a listener and speak only when you have something important to share? There is nothing wrong with doing just that. When it comes to attitudes, you should simply follow what makes you feel authentic.

## How To Be Popular As An Introvert

When you are an introvert, it doesn't automatically mean that you are shy or insecure. Introversion pertains to one's choice to preserve energy instead of being wild and tiring yourself out.

When you are attending a party and when you arrived, you didn't know anyone, just introduce yourself. Simply say "Hi, My name is _____. I don't know anyone here, so I have to introduce myself." Then a fellow guest would reply, "Hello! Nice to meet you. I'm _____." This is a simple way to break the ice.

While you may meet someone friendly, it is also highly likely that you might meet someone unwelcoming. You don't have to worry about them. Just move on and try to mingle with the other guests.

If you meet someone who is nice and confident, they will be more eager to talk to you. It could be the start of a good friendship or even a business partnership.

The more you practice random introduction, the more you can be popular despite the fact that you are introverted.

## Abraham Lincoln - The Introverted Orator

The office of the President of the United States is considered the most powerful position in the free world. Many of us think that individuals who have natural charm and social skills are fit to occupy the White House.

However, many great US presidents were introverted such as Abraham Lincoln. A country-laborer turned self-educated lawyer, Lincoln spent most of his nights reading books, which is one characteristic of introverts.

But despite his introversion, Lincoln realized that he can do more by opposing the injustices during his time. Even without powerful allies, massive wealth, or formal education, the political success of Lincoln seems unlikely. While he is silent most of the time, he was authentic when he needed to press on important matters of the state.

While his political opponents were boisterous and gregarious, he was quiet yet confident and always listening. And when he spoke, it was clear that he was carefully listening.

Lincoln sounded authentic because he had genuine empathy towards his fellow man. Matched with vocal power and knowledge drawn from devouring his books, he was noted as a great communicator.

Whether at public speeches or in private meetings, Lincoln was significantly persuasive by imbuing his every word with the depth that it should be shared and not in the way of a fast-talking extrovert.

## Chapter Conclusion

The first chapter of this book is critical because it establishes authenticity as the overarching theme that is connected with other ways to become more charismatic.

Remember, the real "you" is the best "you", and the "authentic" way is to be what feels genuine for you whether that's being the life of the party or engaging in deep conversations with smaller groups.

People are naturally drawn towards authenticity, and the relationships that you really care about are the ones that will establish the strongest network that you can build.

Be sure that you understand your options and adjust your behavior to reflect your genuine self. When there are things that you really dread doing, try to reframe your mind so you will better understand the significance of accomplishing that task.

The key to being authentic is the ability to look for something in the situation that will allow you to feel genuine and more acceptable.

# Chapter 2 - Build Your Self-Image

In order to establish deeper connections in a more genuine way, you should present the best parts of your authentic self. To put this simply, before you expect others to be attracted to you, you have first to be attracted to yourself.

Chances are, you are already aware of your basic strengths and you can easily exude confidence in different circumstances. However, even the most self-assured person may experience moments of self-doubt. The key is understanding how you can work through them.

Linda is a top sales executive who have experienced moments of self-doubt over the years. She recounted how, as he started garnering recognitions in the company that he would often feel that she just got lucky. Every time, she took these moments of self-doubt as a way to re-evaluate his worth and fortify her self-image by reconnecting with what she knew she could contribute to her workplace.

Over time, she trained himself to embody this awareness. Through a positive self-image, she managed to thrive in her sales career. Many of us are much harder on ourselves than we are on other people.

Is it okay to be judgmental, petty, or mean towards other people? Then, why do you find it okay when you are judgmental, petty, or mean to yourself? Remember, perception is a reality, and self-image is heavily drawn to self-perception.

When you don't follow up with potential clients, because you assume that they will not buy your product, or when you don't pursue a job application because you assume that you are not qualified, you are only affirming your negative assumptions as your reality.
Whenever you are sabotaging yourself with negative thoughts, you have to ask yourself, "Do I really want this client not to buy from me?" If your response is "No" then you have to change your reality.

## The Significance of Self-Image

It can be difficult to make other people believe in your value if you don't even believe in yourself. A negative self-image can significantly affect your decisions, productivity, and personal growth. So why do people hold onto negative self-image?

More often than not, we can gain something when we indulge in negative self-perception. This could be part of our natural instinct to avoid repeating previous mistakes or protecting ourselves against failure. Sometimes, this is also drawn from the desire not to threaten the people around us by challenging the status quo.

Holding yourself back may keep you safe. However, it also means sacrificing how much you can grow and short-changing yourself. Building a positive self-image doesn't necessarily mean that you have to obliterate all doubts and be perfect.

Self-confidence comes from managing your self-doubt and accepting the reality that you are doing something about your flaws, even while understanding these flaws as characteristics that make you likable.

Have you ever had a chance to witness a fashion show? Some outfits are classy, but some are outrageous and out of this world. What are these people thinking? Can you really wear that geometric hat in the workplace? But if you look at the face of the runway models, the attires seemed totally fetching.

Models walk confidently because they know they look good, and they really do. They are completely comfortable, and they show the world that they are likable. As a result, many people admire them. Whatever you think about yourself is who you are.

## Activity: Find the Words to Describe Yourself

This activity is designed to help you find the best words that you can use to define yourself. The words that you can identify will compose the description of your strengths that are not only true but the one you can remember when you are having self-sabotaging thoughts.

### Free Write

- Grab a piece of paper and a pen and for at least 10 minutes, write down all the positive adjectives that you can use to describe yourself. Then think about how you embody or present the qualities you have written.

- Don't use any filters and don't think too much. Just keep writing. If you are stuck, just rewrite the words that you have already written. Just keep the pen moving.
- Don't just concentrate on the qualities that are important for work. Include all aspects of your life. Do your siblings come to you when they have problems because they know you have the right words to say? Do your friends call you when they are having a difficult time because they know you are a reliable friend? Do your neighbors find you easy to talk with because they feel you are a warm person? Write them all down.
- After 10 minutes, stop writing and read what you have written. Then read again.

## Get Feedback

Often, we are blindsided by our own strengths even if they are easily noticed by people around us. So it is crucial to gather information by asking people to describe you.

Make a list of people who really know you well and another list that is composed of your acquaintances.

Then ask these people the following questions (you may also come up with your own set of questions if you want to):

- What's the best word or adjective to describe me?
- What do you think are my best strengths and qualities?

If you are a bit hesitant to ask open-ended questions, you can try presenting characteristics for the person to confirm or deny. Be sure to clarify if you are not clear about or you are surprised by any of the feedback. Why do you think that a particular person chose that word to describe you?

Can that person provide an example of what happened in the past when you have displayed or embodied that characteristic? Make certain that you understand the basis of this comment.

## Consolidate

Take a look at what you wrote about yourself and compare it to the feedback you have collected from others.

Select the words that really resonate with you. The words that you choose are genuine for you.

## Why Are You So Mean to Yourself?

How do you treat yourself? To figure this out, track it for a week and markdown every self-sabotaging thoughts you have. How often do you give yourself a pat on the back when you did really great?

For every scenario, reward yourself a point. In a week, how many times are you mean to yourself? For each scenario, deduct a point. When a thought began as a negative buy you were able to transform that thought into something positive, reward yourself two points.

Tally your points at the end of each week. Where did you end up? Can you increase your points next week? Figure out whether or not you are really happy with your thought patterns. If not, try to be more proactive about changing your self-image and embracing your thoughts.

## Embrace Your Authentic Self

Robert has always wanted to start his own business. For years, he has already made some plans and came up with ideas. However, the venture never materialized because in his head, he had all sorts of reasons why his business would fail.

*"I don't have any business experience."*

*"It's just too hard."*

*"No one will buy your products".*

Robert has always been confident about his strengths, but this didn't stop these thoughts from entering his mind. The effect of his negative self-talk? For years, he failed to take any action at all.

If you are also dreaming of achieving something great - starting your own business, publishing a book, finishing a degree - you have to change your self-perception. It involves the process of continuously reminding yourself that how you plan to succeed in your life is completely up to you.

Changing your perspective about yourself involves actionable steps that can help you reprogram your perceptions and your sense of self-ability so that you have the courage to hustle every day and do the dirty work that you know could help you achieve your dreams.

Self-sabotaging thoughts will not instantly dissipate, and they may never disappear from your life. However, you can successfully take steps so you can manage your negative self-talk and their influence over you. This will free you to accomplish something difficult.

But how can you develop positive images that will help you fight self-sabotaging thoughts? Here are effective techniques that can help you in this process:

## Find a Friend Within

What would you do if you have noticed that one of your closest friends is expressing negative self-thoughts?

Chances are, you would immediately comfort your friend and recite all your friend's amazing characteristics so that the negative thoughts will be transformed from self-sabotaging and damaging to productive and helpful.

Now, what would you do if you have noticed that you are also prone to negative self-thoughts? Can you try becoming a friend for yourself?

Imagine that there are two people behind your back. One is a bully that whispers negative thoughts into your ears, and the other is a cheerleader who reminds you of your goals, strengths, and successes.

When your inner bully begins ranting, stop it immediately and turn to your personal cheerleader.

Don't listen if your bully is shouting "You can't do it, you will never close that sale, you will just stammer, and the client will just insult you!"

Instead, turn to your cheerleader who will say encouraging words to you such as "You have real value that you can offer to this client. You are good at what you do, keeps your promises, and deliver outstanding results. Any client would be lucky to partner with you."

The process can get easier over time. As you increase your awareness of your vulnerability to negative self-thoughts, you can easily catch them, switch on your counterattacks, and become more skilled at changing them into powerful and positive self-image.

## Paint a Positive Picture About Yourself

A key element in countering negative self-thoughts is learning how you can reframe your image from bad to good. It is completely up to you if you see a glass as half-empty or half-full. Whatever your frame of mind, it is totally up to your choice.

If you are focusing your mind on things that you cannot do and the things you are afraid to face, then your results will be significantly affected. Reframing your thoughts could change your perspective from certain failures to resounding success, which affects the results of your decisions and actions. Try to embrace your possibilities and veer away from potential failures.

In reframing your mindset, you need to work on your internal and external self.

With internal framing, you can visualize what you want and then mentally practice how it will happen. You can coach yourself to positively think about your strengths, skills, or your tasks. Positive thinking could lead to positive results.

With external framing, you can choose to take your internal thoughts and express them verbally by sharing them with others to provide them with weight and validity.

Claire was an associate creative director at an advertising agency. She expressed her intention to be a partner, even though she'd been there for only five years and the regular track for the partnership was 10 years.

Rather than giving in to her internal bully shouting "You will just waste your time. They will not consider you as a partner." Claire placed her strong belief in her skills and achieved her goal.

She was confident, determined, and consistent, and has proven her worth. Even though she lacks in the required years, her achievements helped her to become a partner on her 7th year in the agency.

## Celebrate the Small Victories

One of Edward's greatest dreams is to publish a novel. He already had the story in his mind, and he could see the plot. However, the effort required for the caused a massive dosage of inertia to settle in.

He felt that the goal is a lot bigger than him, and he felt overwhelmed. Before he even started writing he wanted to give up.

However, he started breaking down the process into manageable steps, and immediately, he was able to start writing.

Step 1 - Finalize the story plot

Step 2 - Research on the process of publishing a novel

Step 3 - Learn the important elements of the book proposal

Step 4 - Look for a creative editor

Step 5 - Submit manuscripts to different publishing houses

Edward rewarded himself every time he completed a step to mark his enormous relief and sense of accomplishment.

The rewards were not necessarily expensive ones - some were simple as a movie or a pizza - but they helped Edward feel good about achieving his goals and excited to accomplish the next ones.

While working on his novel, Edward's mindset changed from "This is going nowhere!" to "I can do this!"

Progress regardless of how small it is will help you to feel good. It has a significant effect on our thought patterns as well as our productivity and the way we perceive our own image.

## "Fake It Until You Make It"

You are probably wondering why this chapter involves a section about "faking" it. After all, the previous chapter talked about being authentic, and the popular mantra of "fake it until you make it" seems encouraging inauthenticity.

The true purpose of this advice is to try on what it may feel and look like to perceive ourselves in new ways or to act differently than we're accustomed to.

This doesn't mean you have to become a fraud to succeed. Rather, you need to go out of your comfort zone so you can grow comfortable with your changing mindset and until the new reality becomes normal for you.

This is another way to proactively reframe your thoughts as well as your motivations, actions, and decisions.

Fortifying your self-perception is a process, which is crucial to help you improve your charisma.

## What Are You Wearing?

While clothes may not define your character, they are perceived as a reflection of your inner state. If you feel tired and lazy and you dress in shapeless, baggy clothes for comfort, you present that lazy aura to the world.

To be more energetic, try putting on some color in your wardrobe. You will observe that the energy tends to stay with you the entire day and that people will transcend that energy back to you. It can be difficult to be prepared and alert if your clothes are gloomy.

If you are "dressed to kill", other people will perceive you in this manner, which reflects it back to you and fortify the thoughts you have about yourself. Self-perception is the basis of how you see yourself and how other people see you.

## How to Overcome Shyness

Shyness is a natural emotion when we are in a new environment or if we are not comfortable in dealing with a situation (usually a social setting).

However, there are times that shyness can be debilitating that will prevent you from participating in social situations that are crucial for your personal and professional goals. Perhaps, you really want to meet new people or connect with new business contacts, but you are afraid to be criticized or rejected so you avoid social events.

Studies reveal that shyness is sustained through a vicious cycle in which whenever you approach a social setting, you feel excessive fear, and so you avoid the situation that provides you relief. But this usually results in feelings of self-blame and shame.

In order to cope with these feelings, some people turn their negative thoughts into anger and blame, which significantly decreases your likability.

One way to overcome shyness is to plan for an important social situation ahead.

Remember, introversion doesn't mean shyness. The former is associated with your tendency to reserve energy instead of tiring out. On the other hand, shyness is characterized by your strong tendency to overestimate negative criticism.

Shy people tend to become fearful that others will evaluate them in a negative way. More often than not, people who are timid focus on how to avoid committing errors instead of doing things right.

To reduce your anxiety, you need to spend more time thinking about what you can do to become successful.

If you are due to give a presentation, prepare ahead of time and rehearse your slides. This will significantly reduce your shyness knowing that you have studied well to execute the task excellently, but not necessarily perfectly.

Through preparation, you will be more confident because you will be in control.

## Shy Beauty: Nicole Kidman

Nicole Kidman is one of the most recognizable faces on Earth today. She is an award-winning actress and without a doubt oozing with charisma.

But despite her success, she admitted about her shyness. She even stuttered as a kid that she, fortunately, got over and hates going to a party by herself.

To overcome her shyness, Nicole had to practice a lot and come out of her comfort zone. Her shyness in-camera still returns from time to time but manages to deal with it by extensively studying her role.

## Chapter Conclusion

In this chapter, we have explored the importance of self-image in improving your likability.

Before you can expect others to like you, you first need to like yourself. Remember, perception is the reality. How you perceive yourself becomes a reality about you, so be nice to yourself.

Being nice, especially to yourself is not just a fuzzy concept. Studies have shown that positive self-talk can pave the way for success and authentic productivity.

Therefore, it is crucial to transform negative self-talk into a positive one by regularly reminding yourself of your accomplishments in the past. This will help you reframe your challenges or obstacles by building clarity about your intended results and celebrating your small wins.

Learning how to fake it is a powerful way to become more familiar with new thought patterns and strategies. Keep on "faking it" until you can feel your new reality that is outside your comfort zone.

# Chapter 3 - Be Energetic

In any form of social interaction, every person participates in energy transmission that significantly affects the dynamics of social relationships. Becoming more aware of how we feel and act, how the other person feels and acts, and what mixture contributes to our connection is an important tool for improving likability and nurturing meaningful relationships.

More often than not, we are not aware of the energy we emit that affects our communication. As such, we have no idea if the quality of energy we share is working for us or against us.

Recall a situation that went well for you. Can you still remember your mood at that moment as well as how you approach the situation? How can you describe your energy in that scenario? Regardless of how you describe that moment, it will embody the feelings that people around you at that moment were getting from you.

Highly likable people are full of energy, which is derived from your actual mood in a specific moment and your natural personality. You can feel your own energy in the way you stand and in the way you walk or breathe. The people around you can detect this energy signature that is significantly boosted by your choice of words.

Similarly, you can also be affected by other people's energy, which could impact the quality of our interactions. To put it simply, energy is contagious.

Our own energy could energize other people or even cause them to feel down. Your energy can contribute to team productivity or add confusion. Energy can affect the course of communications and paves way for better connections. Your energy during social situations can be picked up by others and affect the result.

Remember, what you give off is what you can get back. Hence, getting your energy to an optimal place before participating in a situation can make all the difference.

It is crucial to tap the energy that can help you in a particular situation. If you understand that energy is something that you create, you can work on controlling your energy rather than having it control you.

It will help you a lot if you know what energy level you should use in a specific situation or when you need to deal with a specific person.

## Using the Right Form of Energy

For other people to perceive you as authentic and sincere, you should be true to yourself and use the right form of energy in a given situation.

It doesn't mean that you have to be loudest in the room. The key here is to be sincere even if you need to face distractions, difficulties, or challenges. This is crucial to effectively connect with people.

Knowing how to transmit the right energy at the right time and in the right place is a critical part of effectively connecting with others. Just don't forget to be authentic.

Before you can understand the right form of energy to use in a given situation, you must first learn how you can be in tune with it. You should know what kind of vibe you are giving off at any moment so you can determine if it is effective or you need to adjust it. Are you currently having difficulty in dealing with your coworker? Try adjusting your approach and bring more open and positive energy to the relationship. Do you find it difficult to motivate your team? Try bringing more energy to the team so they can pick up your vibe, become less combative and achieve some really productive work.

Try to evaluate your energy in a situation and if you think you need to improve, try to adjust. If needed, try tapping into past experiences when you have naturally shared positive energy. You can use these memories so you can change your approach to a new situation or person.

Also, take note that you might need to lead by example. Depending on the energy that other people are contributing to the interaction, it may take some time for them to respond to your energy shift. However, by taking action and calibrating your energy levels, you need to make the first step to bring around more positive results.

Calibrating Your Energy

If you are in a situation where you sense that you are not achieving your intended result, you may calibrate your energy so you can be more open to letting out your more positive and authentic self.

Visualize the emotions that you want to manifest and then recall a memory of a particular time when you have felt that way. Try to recall as many details to make the memory as strong as possible.

Remember the feeling when you have accomplished a task on time and on budget. See the look of admiration from your colleagues. Hear the client comment on the effectiveness of your product.

Try to practice this simple technique, and you will find that your body will relax and you feel more naturally confident and your energy calibrates towards a more positive outlook.

Remember this energy shift with you into the situation you are facing and this is the energy that you can give.

## Detecting Energy Signals of People Around You

To positively affect the energy of a situation, you need to be conscious not only of our energy signals but also the energy signals of other people.

Rate of speech, tone of voice, body language are all indicators of someone's energy signals. A person who is talking fast and heavily sweats gives off a different energy vibe compared to someone who is speaking calmly with arms crossed.

However, you should be open to the fact that you may need clarity in interpreting energy signals.

Crossed arms and downcast look may signal that the person is bored or not interested. But it may also indicate that the person is seriously thinking about a subject. So be sure to ask clarificatory questions if you are not sure of the signals.

Just be careful about your tone and timing when making such clarificatory questions and always use neutral language.

You may use helpful questions such as:

- Is everything okay?
- What do you think about this?
- Can you share what's on your mind?
- Do you want to talk about something?

## Speaking Habits of Likeable People

Not everyone is good at initiating and sustaining good conversations. Our speaking style plays a huge part in making certain that our conversations are exciting yet still relevant.

Is there one winning speaking style that you can follow to demonstrate charm? Unfortunately, there is none. However, you can use the following speaking habits used by people who are well-liked.

## Be Professional

The first thing that you will notice in the way charming people speak is that they are genuinely professional. They will make you comfortable while always maintaining a professional vibe.

Professionalism is a sign of politeness, so the other person will know that you are a respectful person. This is important if you are speaking with a person you just met.

## Avoid Interrupting

This is a classic rule to follow if you want the conversation to be likable. Do not allow yourself to talk if the other person is still talking and making a point. This style will keep the conversation easy and effective.

The habit of butting in will make a massive difference in how you will be perceived by your audience.

## Tell the Truth

It can derail the conversation if you begin referring to things that are obviously not true. If you want to be likable, you need to tell the truth at all times. This will make it so much easier for you to relax and ride along the with the conversation. It will also impact your reputation if you lied to a person then eventually he found out the truth.

## Be Humble

Likable people are humble. It is easy to spot their lack of ego because it stands out so much in the crowd. Someone who is not in the habit of tooting his own horns is a lot more fun to be with than someone who always likes to talk about himself.

## Relax

Chatting with a charming person is easy to follow and naturally enjoyable. This makes a significantly huge difference in terms of how the conversation is going to go. You need to ensure that there's no fear or tension within the conversation, which will provide you the avenue to relax and easily contribute to the conversation.

## Tonality

Tonality is an important aspect of communication and the right tonality can help you become more charismatic. It will help you appear confident, intelligent and the impression that you really know what you are talking about. This attracts attention and allows you to be highly likable.

There's no right tonality for every person and every situation. Rather, you can follow a framework that you can customize to a particular personality type.

## Pitch

Pitch characterizes how high or low your voice is. In order to maximize attention, you can vary your pitch with tonalities depending on the part of your speech. This will also convey excitement or enthusiasm regardless of the topic you are discussing.

If you are trying to make an assertion or a statement, the most effective tonality is to inflect your speech downward. This will convey that you are confident because you say it with conviction instead of seeking approval.

## Volume

If the volume of your voice is too low, people may find it hard to hear you, and others may even dominate your speaking voice. This will not help you assert yourself. While a low voice is usually associated with intimacy and calmness, it lacks the ability to energize the person you are speaking with.

On the other hand, if your voice is too high, people may find you arrogant and rude. Although you may demonstrate enthusiasm, you may struggle to build trust, which is key in likability.

## Pace

According to the National Center for Voice and Speech, the recommended pace of words is 2.5 words per second or 150 words per minute.

If you go beyond this pace, your speech may sound rushed and it becomes stressful to listen, especially if you appear agitated.

Speaking a bit slowly will mean that your points will be better understood but will really annoy people who want to know your statement. This will bore your audience, which is not beneficial to you at all.

Learn how to find the right pace, so you are not a bore but not too fast that you feel agitated.

## Giving a Great Presentation

Thankfully, you can learn how to give a great presentation. With the right guidance and right practice, you can mesmerize your ideas.

Whether you are a creative director pitching your ideas to the client, a start-up founder convincing a potential investor, or a charity organizer asking for donations, you can benefit from the following ideas to help you give a great presentation:

## Frame Your Message

Conceptualizing your message and organizing its structure is an important part of preparing your presentation. Humans are hardwired to respond to stories, so it helps a lot if your message is in a story frame.

You also need to make sure that your story is compelling and will give value to your audience. The goal of your presentation is to ensure that your audience will learn something new or see the world differently afterward.

## Plan Your Presentation

After ensuring that your message is clear and valuable, the next step is to focus on how will you actually present your ideas. People will usually deliver their presentation in four ways:

1. Read the presentation slides or the script from a teleprompter

2.     Prepare bullet points that will help you map out what you want to say in each section

3.     Memorize your talk verbatim or word for word

4.     Familiarize yourself with the core message and deliver it from your heart

The fourth one is the ideal way to deliver your presentation as you can engage your audience and you will really present your authentic self.

## Be Comfortable with the Stage

For novice presenters, the idea of facing a crowd can be nerve-wracking. However, experts say that many of us have the tendency to overthink this aspect.

Your success or failure as a presenter will depend on how you are able to make your audience listen to you and how you can make them understand your message, not on how nervous you are. In addition, stage presence is something that you can learn with a bit of coaching.

You don't need to move around. Stand still and use hand gestures to make your point or emphasize an important part of your presentation.

Another important aspect of stage presence is making eye contact. Whenever you are giving a presentation, try to find three to four people in the audience and look them in the eyes.

Eye contact is surprisingly powerful, and this will help you drive your point more than any theatrics.

Take note that there's no good way to deliver a presentation. The most memorable presentations offer a fresh and unique perspective on an idea. The most boring ones are those that are too generic.

However, it may be difficult to find openers that are dependent on the person or situation, especially if you are meeting someone for the first time. There are several generic fallback questions you may use in such situations, so you can use them if needed.

At first, the responses of your conversation partner may sound unenergetic, because most of these questions are quite a cliché already. Nevertheless, you can use responses to determine interesting details about the person.

## What do you do?

Even though this one is quite overused, it is also proven effective in initiating conversations. This is a generic question that you can ask anyone.

If you are talking to someone who has retired or whose employment status is not known, you can instead ask "What field you are in?"

In asking this question, you must listen and understand the answer. You really need to hear what the person is saying. Try to find out what value you can offer through his responses and always follow up with new questions.

If they are professionals, you may ask how did they choose their field? If they have their own business, ask what was it like to start as an entrepreneur?

As you will see, the possibilities for engaging in a deeper conversation are quite endless.

All you need to do is to follow your curiosity. If someone asks you the same questions, you should take the chance to open up.

## What do you think of the weather?

Another generic conversation starter is to ask about the weather. This icebreaker can lead to trivial small talk or it may result in more valuable connections.

The response may lead to a conversation about the comparisons of the weather in the person's hometown or the challenges of working in deep winter.

It may lead to dialogue about favorite vacation spots or what's the ideal weather for a specific business. Begin with a standard question and be ready to pursue further conversations based on the person's responses.

## Sustaining Conversations

To sustain an engaged conversation, you have to learn how to politely probe. A probe is a type of question, which digs deeper into the topic. Probing is useful in exploring new materials for conversations.

Regardless of your curiosity and a long list of follow-up questions, there will be instances in conversations that you will suddenly hit a brick wall. If this happens, it is best to follow the lead of the person that you are trying to engage in a conversation.

If you tried to probe a topic and the other person lost enthusiasm, find a new topic until you find a new one that can help in the dialogue flow again. The more energetic replies you can get, the better your chances for sustaining to probe in ways that can harness connection.

There are three types of probing questions: expansion questions, rational questions, and clarifying questions.

## Expansion Questions

These questions are also known as elaboration questions because they delve for more information about a specific response. One popular expansion question is "Can you tell me more?"

This question may invite people to elaborate on something that is interesting to them that naturally makes them feel more comfortable.

It will also allow the people you want to engage with to know that you are really interested in knowing what they are discussing. This places them at ease that they are not dominating the conversation.

Expansion questions will provide you more opportunities to listen and learn the genuine interests, needs, and concerns of the other person and how you may be able to help.

## Rational Questions

Rational questions are mainly used to understand the reason behind a stated choice or action. But instead of asking "Why?" you should instead use the question "How come?"

Regardless of your intention, "why" is a word that can easily put the other person on the defensive. This makes people feel as if they are placed on the hot seat and should defend their answers.

On the other hand "How come?" poses a more authentic inquiry that reduces the possibility that the question will be received as some kind of attack. You should also try to watch your rate of speech and tone of voice.

Longer probes like "I'm really curious, what made you let go of your job to start your own business?" feels more genuine and less aggressive compared to a generic and lightning-fast "How come?"

## Clarifying Questions

Clarifying questions will show that you are paying attention to the person you are talking with. Summarize or rephrase what you have heard and ask if you really got it, or if you don't think that you have understood, be sure to ask the person to provide more details.

Clarifying questions are also great conversation stallers because they will buy you time if you are thinking about where you want to take the conversation next. But be careful how you phrase your clarifying questions.

Stay away from openers like "Are you saying...?" that, depending on your tone and whom you are talking to, can be wrongly received as outrage, judgment, or shock.

Rather, you can paraphrase what you think you heard and then check if you really got it right.

## Never Interrogate

When you are probing, be sure not to interrogate the person. Never ask any questions unless you really want to know the answer. Chances are, you will just tune out if the other person replies and you really don't care.

If you ask something that genuinely interests you, the follow-up questions will come naturally and your body language, as well as energy, will reflect your interests. Just be careful not to let your enthusiasm tip over into a rapid-fire.

Firing people with machine-gun questions, regardless of your exuberance, may make them feel as if they have to defend themselves, so they will do so.

Take note that conversations are two-sided, filled with breaks and spontaneous chats during which the people talking with each other consider and absorb what is being discussed.

Opening up and sharing information about yourself is also critical because it helps in building a bond that good communication can harness. This makes you more charismatic and makes people around you comfortable enough to share.

## Chapter Conclusion

In this chapter, we have explored the importance of curiosity in harnessing our charisma. This can be done by engaging in meaningful conversations that can be sustained by asking the right questions.

In conversations, we appear more comfortable and authentic if you remain curious. You can do this even without deeper knowledge of the person you are speaking with.

Curiosity will bring out the best in you and will prompt you to naturally do all the things that can foster positive connections.

# Chapter 4 - Cherish Similarities and Honor Differences

Learning that we share a connection with a person can help us to be more comfortable, regardless of the connection is trivial or a more serious one. The similarities might be having mutual friends, liking the same food, or have had similar experiences.

Realizing those genuine similarities as well as associations could increase your ease with new people, and also, their comfort with you. Being comfortable not only makes communication easier but can also open new windows to discover new things. This is key to building more meaningful connections.

At first, the similarities we have with people may not be obvious. However, learning how to stay alert to these commonalities is part of the work of establishing connections into deeper relationships.

As we pursue our careers, we often cease finding similarities with people we know. We may think we have already learned all the information we need about them.

Taking a closer look at our existing relationships is another helpful approach to continue nurturing our relationships. This includes relearning our curiosity about the people we know and staying conscious of the things we may share aside from the task at hand.

## The Importance of Likability

Our level of comfort increases when we meet someone with whom we have strong commonalities. Our charm becomes effective as the conversation flows naturally.

In general, people tend to like people who are like them. Of course, this doesn't mean that you can magically sense this whenever you meet someone. There are just instances that the commonalities are too strong, and you may also come up against the same characteristics that you may not like.

In such instances, it is ideal that you step back if you can and evaluate your resistance. There are also instances that the commonalities are direct and explicit, and sometimes they are more subtle that can only be detected over time.

But once we discover our commonalities, we can build opportunities for more meaningful and more genuine relationships. The path towards likability can become shorter and smoother. As the comfort level increases, communication becomes more open that builds more trust.

While you can't automatically achieve likability, you can easily start building it by finding similarities.

## Trust and Likability

We usually trust other people in our line of work to recommend a vendor or a product. We often shortlist a candidate for a job because a trusted colleague had a positive experience in working with that person in the past.

Trust is a key element in likability because people trust the sources they really know best. This is the same principle behind your willingness to go on a blind date arranged by someone you really know. In your mind, "Roger knows her, and Roger knows me, so I can trust that at the least, she's a decent, normal lady."

This is also the reason why many companies are fond of offering referral programs. If a company already has employees whom they genuinely trust, then it is easy to tap this resource in looking for new staff members.

Validating our choices is important for harnessing likability. We connect to a person or a brand through a third party that we trust. We ask our neighbors for the number of a good gardener. We ask colleagues with similar tasks for tool recommendations. We trust parents with kids the same age as ours for advice about pediatricians and tutors. If our friend trusts a particular person, we find it easy to like that person, too.

## Discovering Similarities

There are numerous ways we can be associated or similar to another person. This point can be easily illustrated through social media sites such as Facebook. How many degrees of separation are you away from people you don't know? Try to use Facebook to search for people you share the same name who are living in your suburb.

Chances are, you will see several people who have the same first name as you who are living nearby, and some of them know people who are in your list of friends.

Similarities are all around us, even if they are not obvious at first. Having mutual friends is just one way to increase your likability. We may learn other areas of commonality as well like common experience, work histories, shared educational backgrounds, demographic similarities, and shared values and beliefs. All these are possible ways to create the basis for genuine connection.

When we first meet someone, we often ask generic questions such as:
- Where do you work?
- Where did you grow up?
- Where did you go to school?

Learning information that matches our own can easily increase our interest and excitement in the new person. Finding the similarity could easily lead to sustained conversation and will result in deeper connection.

Commonalities that may not be obvious at first can come to the surface easily with the right types of questions. Avoid interrogating someone by rapid-fire questions. Be sure that you also share important aspects of yourself.

Self-disclosure is crucial if commonalities are going to be effectively discovered. You may mention your organizational affiliations, places you have lived, your interests or hobbies.

You can also allow the other person to discover similarities by learning about their backgrounds and interests as well as finding common territories. With this, you can further harness your capacity to build stronger relationships. The more information you know about the person, the stronger the foundation you can build on.

## Shared Passion

Shared passion can bring people together in ways that are stronger compared to other relationships. If we are passionate about a specific interest, the experience is emotionally powerful. The connection can be intense and fast if you share the same feelings with a person.

If you are a dog parent and you see someone who loves his canine friend, you can easily feel the same passion as that person. There are times that these shared beliefs are quite apparent because of the context in which you meet - at a park walking your pets, at a house of worship, or an industry conference.

In some instances, you may need to ask questions to determine if you have shared passion. Below are some questions that you can ask to figure out if there are potential connections you can find through shared passion:

- I am interested in sharing my time and talent as a volunteer in a local organization. Can you recommend a local charity or civic group?
- We just moved to the neighborhood. Can you recommend a place to unwind?
- What do you think about the current city mayor?

- Are you happy with our congressman's recent actions?
- Can you recommend a local church or temple?

Religion and politics are two subjects that many people feel passionate about. So these are interesting areas that you can explore. Just be sensitive about intense emotions and try to consider changing the topic or backing off if the conversations become too heated.

Remember, your goal is to establish a connection and not find an enemy.

## The Art of Mirroring

Some commonalities are easy to see such as an action or a way of speaking. When we feel at ease in a situation, we mirror back those things when we communicate in some way.

This is usually done unconsciously but a distinct way we can relate when they feel connected.

Mirroring usually happens without thinking. However, it can also be used in conscious methods to provide more comfort to a situation or express understanding. If a person is telling you something excitedly, leaning forward in his chair, it may also help communicate your interest if you use body language that mirrors this behavior. So, you may also lean forward.

On the other hand, leaning away could indicate detachment, which is the exact opposite of what we are after. Leaning forward builds a similarity that could lead to better understanding.

It will feel natural even if you are aware that you are mirroring someone else's action. However, forcing it will be too obvious. Don't overdo it. Just be aware how you are genuinely experiencing the conversation and allow your movements to mirror the engagement.

## Similarities Could Help Set the Mood

If you want to be more likeable, it is ideal to look for similarities when you are meeting new people. It will help you to build trust, wherever and whatever those commonalities might be. As we pursue our careers, we may experience narrowing down our repertoire for dealing with new situations. So, it is crucial to keep harnessing our social skills.

Ask questions so you can be attuned to the wide range of information you receive in response. There are a lot of ways that you may connect with someone, and through genuine curiosity and listening skills, you may discover what you have in common with someone and where your genuine connections happen.

Similarities build the foundations for trust if you are forging new relationships. Just as it is essential to figure out similarities to help in establishing genuine comfort in personal relationships, it is important to end a conversation with those feelings of trust.

## How to Be Charming Without Trying

There are people who seem naturally charming. Whatever they do (even if they are not doing anything) they are perceived to be as charming.

People are naturally drawn to them, and they are very fun to be with.

It can be hard to fake your behavior so more people will like you. In order to be charming without trying, you should be authentic.

Remember, being genuine makes you likeable. Be genuinely curious about people, and if you are really curious, make certain that you are polite.

Unfortunately, there are people who are curious but could be intrusive. Yes, you may ask questions, but never interrogate the person as if you are trying to extract the truth.

Another simple way to be charming without too much effort is to smile. This easy gesture can make you appear more attractive instantly.

Happiness is an attractive feature in both men and women who are highly charismatic. Those who are naturally happy and always smiling are like magnets that attract people. So smile so you can feel better about everything in your life.

## Chapter Conclusion

In this chapter, we have explored the importance of finding similarities to increase our likability. Remember, people like people who are like them.

In the same vein, people trust people they know best. Being affiliated with a trusted source will usually mean that this element of trust can be transferred to you.

Discovering similarities is also key to improve our charisma. Try to determine common backgrounds and interests, shared experiences and beliefs to look for similarities that could help you in building connections with other people.

The subtle art of mirroring can also help you harness your likability. If you are comfortable in a conversation and you feel engaged, you can communicate this by reflecting it through your body language.

# Chapter 5 - Give Value

One of the best ways to become charismatic and build a connection is to show that we understand the needs of other people, and we are happy to fulfill them.

By using the lessons you have learned in the previous chapters, you can be creative to expand the types of value we can offer to other people.

In most instances, people are willing to share, because they are expecting something in return. However, you can provide genuine value if you learn how to give simply because you want to.

Sharing creates value, which doesn't always mean making grand gestures or exerting major effort.

Even in your own little ways, you can send a clear signal that you are thinking about the other person and that you are genuinely interested to help.

More often than not, it is easy to see how you can help a person. Sometimes, it is not obvious, especially if the person is far more superior than you.

However, everyone needs and appreciates a helping hand. Regardless of your status in life, you can always bring value to someone else.

Providing assistance is one of the best ways to increase your charisma as it opens the door to building the relationship.

With each interaction, you can increase your similarity and familiarity.

## How to Provide Value to Another Person

There are endless ways to bring value to another person, and anyone has something to offer.

Whether it's by offering feedback and support, building opportunities for meaningful interactions, or sharing resources, you can always share by finding more opportunities to give back.

People have the tendency to react to situations in the same manner that works on a particular level. If something has worked out in the past, there's a big chance that it will be effective again in the future. However, sticking only to the proven methods can narrow down our perspective of what we are capable of doing for other people.

Probably, we feel as if we don't have the time and the resources to share. Sometimes, we are not sure if giving will be appropriate.

By widening our perspectives and broadening our creativity in handling situations, we can understand that sharing is a continuous process and can benefit you throughout your career.

In seeking opportunities to help other people, you can identify all the ways that can bring value to your relationships.

## Personal and Business Connections

One way to bring value to another person is to be a matchmaker. When you meet someone, try thinking about other people whom they might be interested to meet.

When you become a matchmaker, you can leverage all other lessons you have learned in this book.

You can be curious about the person, and then your interest will be awakened if you identify commonalities.

Before you introduce people, you should always ask them if they want to be introduced, because you should only connect people if they are both interested.

You should also be mindful that introductions can also affect the reputation of a person, so it is best to be careful about this.

By establishing connections between two people for whatever reason, you can create meaningful interactions that will further increase your likability.

## How To Be The "Cool One"

Contrary to the common belief, being "cool" is not about you, but it is about other people.

This involves their expectations and perceptions. Here are a few things you should know if you want to be perceived as a cool person.

### Wear Proper Clothes

If you are not conscious about how you wear your clothes, other people may take you for a slob who doesn't take yourself seriously.

Just think about the cool people you know, and how they dress properly to set the expectation.

Some guy with messy hair walks into a conference wearing a black shirt, a pair of rugged blue jeans, and wearing a dirty pair of sneakers. What do you think about this guy?

*Probably like "Man, this person is an outsider".*

You might be an interesting person, but very few people will actually give you their attention just because you failed to live up to the expectation of a cool person.

So does this mean we need to wear a tuxedo? Now, that's ridiculous. Formal wear has their purpose, but so do jeans and shirts.

If you want to be the coolest guy in the room, you need to wear clothes that are suitable for the environment.

## Be Interesting

Cool people are really interesting. Certainly, it may be difficult to tell if you're really interesting or if the other person is just really polite. However, it is quite easy to tell the difference.

If the other person finds you interesting, they will ask questions to look for more information. If they are just nodding, then you can't say that they are really into you.

Moreover, if they move closer to you, then there's a good chance that the person finds you interesting. Of course, this could be because they want to hear you better, but psychologists reveal that this is actually a subconscious signal that they really find you interesting.

## Use the Appropriate Body Language

As you will later learn in the next chapter, nonverbal communication such as body language can be used to become more likeable.

If you want to convey that you are a cool person, do not cross your arms as this indicates that you are closed off and you are not willing to engage in any conversation.

For you to become the coolest guy in the room, you should learn how to use your body language to your benefit.

How can you achieve this? You can smile, laugh, and use kind gestures. Use the right tonality of your voice that is proper for your environment. Convey your charm through your posture and movements.

Being the coolest person in the room is not something that you can master in a few days, but it can be achieved.

With the tips discussed above, and regular practice, you can really enhance your charisma to help you achieve your business and personal goals.

## Chapter Conclusion

Learning how you can provide value to the people you engage with is key in improving your likability. Learn how to give, because you can and because this act brings value to the relationship that you are trying to establish.

There are many ways that you can bring value to other people such as playing matchmaker to people who may mutually benefit from each other, giving advice, doing favors, sharing resources, and extending invitations to interesting activities and events.

Try to be proactive in determining how you could help the people in your social circle. You can do this by making an action plan that details what you need to do, who you will do it for, and when you want to make that plan happen.

Always remember in the law of karma - what comes around, goes around. You will reap rewards in return, if you have the habit of giving.

You will significantly increase your chances to be a likeable person if you know how to pay it forward. You can repay the generosity you have received by continuing the chain.

# Chapter 6 - Be Memorable

**W**ho is your closest friend? Try to visualize the last time you spent time with this friend. How does this particular memory make you feel? Do you feel great about just thinking about it?

Now, think about a conversation you had recently that didn't go so well. Maybe you were cornered at the office by an annoying colleague or you got trapped in a conversation with someone who was really creepy at a bar. Think about having to meet that person again.

The way you experience a situation or a person - the emotions you feel, whether positive or negative - could still linger in your memory.

Experts call this mood memory, which is the impression or emotion you associate with a person or a particular event. A key part of improving your charisma is creating positive memories of yourself to other people.

Surprisingly, it's not totally what you said that can bring happy memories to a person. Try to think about a person that really makes you feel good. Can you remember a conversation with this person? Probably. But it can be difficult to remember the conversation.

Was it the general outlook on things or the person's mannerisms? Even if you can't figure out the exact reasons why you feel good when you remember that person, you just feel good about it all. People will remember you more on how you made them feel than what you have said.

The person who can naturally tell jokes without being offensive can leave everyone in a more positive mood. However, the person who always dismisses your ideas and often rude can bring negative energy.

Memories are encoded not only as sensory information but also as emotional information. This is why whenever we recall a memory, we usually find ourselves reminiscing the feelings we experienced when it first happened.

The lingering remembrance of feeling (the positive memory) is important of charisma. If people have a positive mood memory of you, they will be happy to hang out with you or do business with you.

# Jokes That Make People Instantly Like You (Ellen DeGeneres Style)

Ellen DeGeneres is one of the funniest celebrities today. By learning from her wit and humor, you can learn the proper way to joke around so people will find your likable and not offensive.

By using the right form of humor, you can easily win people over and create the right impression by making them smile or even laugh.

According to experts, Ellen employs three kinds of jokes that disarms her guests and make them like her instantly. Read on and find out if you can also use these jokes to enhance your charisma.

## 1. Ego Booster Jokes

Don't you love it when someone compliments you? But instead of direct compliment, you can instead inject some humor.

In one awards night, Ellen was hosting the show and said to Amy Adams who received several nominations for two films:

"...that's so (what's the word for it) selfish."

People will instantly like you if you make them laugh while also highlighting their success.

## 2. Poking Fun Jokes

One perfect example of this joke is when Jennifer Lopez was a guest on Ellen's show.

Jennifer shared that she had bronchitis, and then later on when the star touched Ellen, the comedienne reached for a tissue to wipe her hands as if her guest gave her bacteria.

Even though that joke was poking fun of Jennifer's bronchitis, it was totally in good faith as it didn't alienate the guest because there's no harm in the fact that she got sick.

However, you need to be careful in cracking this type of joke. Be sensitive as some people are insecure if you poke fun of things that are core to their identity or if you are making fun of something that is permanent.

For example, don't make fun of people who have abnormal gait as it is really offensive and could be perceived in bad taste.

## Self-Deprecating Jokes

Jokes that are meant to ridicule yourself are usually harmless. For example, when Rihanna was a guest at Ellen's show, the host asked her about her birth year. When Ellen learned that it was 1988, Ellen playfully replied, "I still have shoes from '88", which implies that she was already old.

Making fun of yourself is an effective way to make people like you. You may make fun of other people but be careful to only do this to your closest friends. It is usually not okay to make fun of people you just met, especially in a business setting.

# Use Your Energy, Body, and Words

In the previous chapters, we have explored how our choices of words, body language and energy could affect not only our perception of ourselves but also the perception of other people on us. These elements are crucial to position your image as a positive one.

The energy that enters a situation could dictate your choices of words as well as body language. These elements transfer your energy to other people that in turn affects their memory about you and the situation. This is a cycle and one that you can easily affect you when you are conscious.

## Energy Transfer

Bear in mind that energy is contagious. If you really want to make others feel good, you should also feel good. This doesn't mean that you should always be happy. You just need to connect with what feels positive and proper in the situation as well as the person you need to deal with.

When you are aware of this, you can consciously shift your level of energy to fit a particular situation. Consider what energy will work best for you at that moment, and if needed, try to remember a time when you were energetic.

Concentrate on as many details as you can to remember what it felt like, and try to internalize it. The key is not to fake the mood but instead, find or re-create the mood within yourself.

## Body Language

According to Albert Mehrabian, a renowned psychologist, body language contributes more than 50% to our charisma.

If you want your genuine image to linger with someone after the conversation, you must make certain that what you say during the interaction is true with how you say it.

Your verbal, as well as non-verbal messages, should communicate with the same things. There are many subtleties in body language.

It is often challenging to learn the rules for non-verbal communication because of the variables in style, gender, and cultural differences. However, there are some general ways you can communicate through your gestures that are important to focus on.

Be mindful of the following aspects of body language if you wish to increase the potential for building positive memories:

## Smiling

There's power in a genuine smile. It can convey openness, trustworthiness, and approachability. Perhaps, this is the single most immediate way to communicate likability. A genuine smile can build strong positive mood memories. People can remember your smile even if they cannot remember what you've said.

You can use your smile as an invitation to engage a conversation and feel comfortable saying what is really in your mind. Not all of us can naturally smile, but this can be achieved through practice. Gradually, muscle memory will take over and it will be easier for you to naturally smile.

## Eye Contact

Consistent eye contact can make a person feel respected and listened to. There is numerous research that provides veracity to this claim. Direct eye contact can release feel-good endorphins and the heart begins to beat a bit faster.

Of course, this doesn't mean that you should be staring at someone relentlessly. The goal is to be charismatic and not to be creepy. Just follow your natural instincts to sustain eye contact to show that you are listening and understanding what the other person is saying.

## Nodding

Nodding is another powerful non-verbal signal, albeit can be specific to gender. Body language experts suggest that women nod to show that they are listening, while men nod if they agree with something.

Regardless if you are a man or a woman, you should be conscious of how much you are doing it. Remember, nodding should be a non-verbal cue.

Overdoing this non-verbal signal will defeat its purpose. In the same vein, paying attention to when you must nod may actually help you convey how much you are experiencing the situation.

Nodding can effectively convey that you understand what you are hearing especially if backed up by quick verbal signals such as "I agree with you" or "That's really interesting".

## Personal Space

Personal space refers to the physical distance between two people when they are in a conversation. There are two primary things that can affect how a person feels about personal space: communication style and culture.

In some cultures, such as in India, they are comfortable with intimacy. It is okay with friends to hold each other even if they are just casually talking. On the other hand, some cultures in Northern Europe such as in Finland, people prefer to maintain more distance.

If you go to India, you will commonly see groups of male friends walking together with arms draped around each other or even holding hands. If you travel to Finland, you will see people standing a bit apart.

## **Word Choice**

Bear in mind that the words we use—in thinking or in speaking— are our choice that reflects the way we think. Using positive frames can help you stick to your genuine thoughts while providing you the opportunity to express them in a positive light.

Be conscious of your word choice, and always make sure to be positive.

"I don't have the easiest job."

This sentence alone is a good example of positive word choice.

"I have a difficult job."

Now, that sentence is basically synonymous with the first one. However, there's a significant difference between the two methods of framing the essential fact.

By choosing to say you don't have the easiest job, you can make it easy for the next thought to be "But it isn't the most difficult job, either."

Choosing this method can immediately direct your thinking to the positive and balances of energy that are more neutral.

Aside from word choice, you also need to express your thoughts. This is an effective way to manage internal distractions and increase your listening capacity.

The key is to not allow people to misinterpret what's going on in your mind if you can just tell them.

## Ask For Advice

Conveying your authentic interest in someone by following your natural curiosity could help in building connections and open more opportunities to improve relationships.

To be more memorable, talk to the people you really admire and ask for advice. When you ask someone for their expertise or advice, you are sending a message that you value that person.

This builds a positive memory because people basically feel recognized and respected for their strengths when other people are seeking advice from them. Similarly, you are leveraging your curiosity and building opportunities to learn. Seeking out advice could leave you vulnerable, but eventually, you can use this for your own benefit.

Being vulnerable is being open and genuine, which are charming traits. By having the confidence to expose yourself, you can open up the door for sustained communication. In business settings, mentor-mentee dynamics is a classic advice-seeking relationship.

This connection could be effectively developed with someone you already know. But you can also try to set this connection with people you just met for the first time.

As a mentee, you may feel that you are taking more value than what you can offer. This is okay as eventually, you will have your chance to provide value to your mentor.

Also, bear in mind that people really like to be recognized and valued for their expertise. By asking for advice, you can create a positive mood memory that helps in sustaining relationships so that it will continue to evolve.

## How to End a Conversation

It is not always easy to know when to end a conversation. Ending it too soon may convey the message that you are not interested, or you would rather be talking to someone else or do something else.

On the other hand, talking out too long may create the impression that you don't respect the time of the other person or you are not sensitive to the subtle signals that the other person wants to go out of the conversation.

Try to leave the conversation with the other person yearning a bit more of you and feeling energized from the interaction. If you have the power to read people's minds as you ending the conversation, ideally, you will think something like this:

- "It was nice to talk to you; I hope to meet you again, soon."
- "I'm ecstatic that you asked for my advice. It gave me an opportunity to help, and it made me feel valued and recognized."

If you are not sure if you want to end the conversation, you can try the following subtle tactics, which can provide the other person a chance to stop the conversation or continue if they want to.

- "Can I grab you a drink?" - This conversation curtailer can create an easy way to the exit. You may say "I'm getting myself a drink; do you want one?". This will allow for both possibilities - continuation or exit. Learn how to take a cue from the response of the person.

- "Should we mingle? This one is applicable to almost any situation. Joining a crowd with someone else can create opportunities to re-energize the conversation or open up new subjects to discuss.

- "I need to go there." This approach is quite useful in a workshop or conference setting. You can try saying "I want to go check out that booth, do you like to join me?" It conveys that you are not trying to get rid of the person because you are even open to the possibility of exploring more of the conference with him.

Before ending the conversation, try to make the other person feel good and try to ask for another chance to reconnect. Ending the conversation with a good impression will leave the door open so you can follow up with the person. Many conversations naturally end, with or without the help of any conversation ender.

In such cases, if it is clear that it is time to end the conversation, you can pair your words with body language. This includes picking up your bad, looking at your watch, putting on your coat, or extending your arm for a handshake.

Basically, being memorable is all about creating a positive impression. There are numerous ways to be memorable, but the most effective one is always show your authentic self.

## Chapter Conclusion

In this chapter, we have explored the importance of leaving a positive impression to enhance your charisma.

Always remember that people are more willing to remember how you made them feel compared to what you said.

The energy you share usually has more of a lasting impression on someone compared to the exact words you have said.

In improving your charisma, you can use effective word choices, body language, and energy shifts. How you perceive and present yourself can significantly affect the impression you leave.

# Conclusion

Charisma is more than a cheeky idea or a concept of which you must stay conscious - it is an outlook to your life and the people around you.

The point of harnessing your likability is not for you to be agreeable to everyone and for everyone to be agreeable with you. Rather, the point is to build valuable connections that could help your productivity, your social health, your relationships, and the quality of your life.

Be genuine in your interactions and follow what you really want to do and not what you think you must do. Even though the overarching principle was discussed in Chapter 1 - Be Authentic - this book is not intended for linear understanding. All the methods described in this guide are intertwined and can work in harmony with one another.

Based on how you want your relationships to succeed and where you are in your career, you can focus on each method that will be most valuable for you at present.

Select one and work on integrating this into your interactions with the people around you. Eventually, that approach will be second nature to you, and so you can move on to the next approach to focus on.

If you enjoyed this book, please take the time to leave me a review where you purchased this book from.

I appreciate your honest feedback, and it really helps me to continue producing high-quality books.

Best wishes

*Darcy Carter*

# Buyer Bonus:

## Rituals Of The Rich & Famous

Free Access to Success Tips, Strategies and Habits of The Rich & Famous

Join successful subscribers!

Get 4 new strategies every week on how to be more charismatic, confident, and happy.

### Free Sign Up Here

# Buyer Bonus 2

## Attachment Theory, The Science of Successful Relationships, Authentic Love, Romance and Connection

Discover the secrets to building healthy, happy, and rewarding relationships.

The key ingredient to happy and fulfilled people is the quality of their intimate, social, family, and professional relationships - nothing else in life comes even remotely close.

Go ahead, transform the quality of your relationships and make love work for you.

# ATTACHMENT THEORY

*The Science of Successful Relationships, Authentic Love, Romance and Connection*

**DARCY CARTER**

www.ingramcontent.com/pod-product-compliance
Lightning Source LLC
Chambersburg PA
CBHW031124080526
44587CB00011B/1101